Take Your Faith UP!

14 Days of Uplifting Word

*14 Promises to Fuel
Your Prayer Life*

R.L. Toney

Encourage Yourself

Take your strength from the well of all living things.

It would seem when things - so much is taken from you, you have
a decision to make. Surrender to it all or take what's yours back.

By sheer force of will, or out of simple desperation; faith draws
on the promise to be. Yielding nothing in its reach, as it grows
it draws the weight necessary to hold it down as the storms and
towering threats emerge to test its state. Do you believe? Will you
stand?
It shall be seen.
It shall be shown as only life can.

1st Samuel 30:6 (TLB)
But David took strength from the Lord.

A Word of Faith:

I look up to the mountains;
does my strength come from mountains?
No, my strength comes from God,
who made heaven, and earth, and mountains.
He won't let you stumble,
your Guardian God won't fall asleep.
Not on your life! Israel's
Guardian will never doze or sleep.
God's your Guardian,
right at your side to protect you—
Shielding you from sunstroke,
sheltering you from moonstroke.
God guards you from every evil,
he guards your very life.
He guards you when you leave and when you return,
he guards you now, he guards you always.

Psalm 121
The Message

7

Pure

Before we begin this journey you should know, to me, faith is a simple word. Borne with a hefty meaning, it requires help to make it work. Believe yes, but action is the part (on your part) that is required.

Believe in the power, in yourself, that foundation is pretty well set. Trust the knowledge and where it leads, that's been told. To see it to its end — now you have to go.

In the face of difficulties — circumstances and conditions which you don't feel prepared for, the action of your part is required... you are necessary. You have to make it happen.

A simple thought comes to mind.

All things, not God, are subject to change.

Contents

Let encouragement end and begin with Day 1

Publish Your Position

Of what importance is the human race, that you should notice them? ...you appoint
them to rule over your creation; you have placed everything under their authority,
Psalm 8:4 -6 (NET)

* * *

Begin today emboldened. Empowered by a process that begin
before you were created to possess the world. Though we
technically gave it all away, by faith it has been restored to us.
Speak it. Loudly if necessary! Tell the world of your faith. Tell the
world of your high status. Let the world know - you are God's
Child!

This day and every day begin it with a simple thought — man has
power. You are empowered. Gifted, anointed; divinely attributed
status. The first step in your true beginning is to recognize it and
say it aloud. Announce it to the world — to yourself. You belong to
God!

Fix your thoughts and behavior on the change you wish to see in
your life and remember, it is written. It is written and therefore
already decided you have authority. God given; Confirmed in
Jesus. You have the power to change your world you simply need
to affirm it (to yourself) and exercise it. Begin your day with - I am
God's Child. What he speaks of me, I speak of me and expect to

see in my life.

Things to know and do:

You are Heir (Joint Heir) apparent.
Commit to a decision.
Discover your voice and use it.

Prayer:

Dear God/ Holy Father, open my eyes and ears to the discovery of who I am in you. Help me, I pray, to then be bold in giving, discussing, bringing it to others so that we may truly meet and be as one body of faith in Christ Jesus. In whose name I pray. Amen!

More of Him

Genesis 1:27 | Psalm 8:6 | Luke 10:19 | 1st Corinthians 11:3 | 1st Corinthians 15:27 | Ephesians 1:22

Judge and Consider

Keep in mind that the LORD your God is [the only] God. He is a faithful God, who keeps his promise and is merciful to thousands of generations of those who love him and obey his commands. Deuteronomy 7:9 (NIV)

* * *

Who do you believe in? What is your core foundation? It's time today to commit to a decision.

Do you trust God? Do you want to exercise faith? Trusting God is easily said but what it means; putting aside the ways of the world and the thoughts it has. It means removing the barriers and stepping into a new supercharged forever. Seeing things from an eternal perspective — with a renewed focus. Christian (believer), it is already settled.

God's word is settled. His plan has borne (is bearing) fruit. The foundations of the world - the hope of a better tomorrow are set and settled - ready to be accepted by you.

Do you disbelieve? Walking with his promises, walking in his truth...

His promises, you know, are immutable. Even with tampering they are indisputable. They are happening and going to happen. You will see them in Christ if you see them in Christ. Remember Noah's rainbow.

He gave his son as a blessed rainbow - a sign, a symbol; an eternal hope but not hope as it's recently defined. Hope, that believers of old had that, (His promises) are already settled (in effect). It's going to happen. The decision is, will you be a part of it?

Things to know and do:

Where or with whom do you place your faith?
Have you experienced His trustworthiness?
What is your Hope?
What has He said to you?

Prayer:

Lord I believe. Help me, my unbelief.

More of Him

Genesis 9:17 | Numbers 23:19 | Psalm 89:34 | Psalm 119:89 | Hebrews 6:18 | 1st Thess. 5:24

Commit Yourself

So let what I'm saying sink deeply into your hearts and souls. Do whatever it takes to remember what I'm telling you: tie a reminder on your hand or put a reminder on your forehead where you'll see it all the time, and on the doorpost where you cross the threshold or on the city gate. Deuteronomy 11:18 (VOICE)

* * *

Devoting your ways and means to an idea is a big ask. Perhaps no bigger than giving your all for a people that don't know you. Nevertheless the reality is all the promises of God are true and freely given; to be shared. Regardless of feeling he offers them, they are sought after... yet unavailable to many because of lack of knowledge of them.

What you don't know you won't attain. It doesn't help you. You can't effectively experience goodness even when you experience goodness. You don't recognize it because it hasn't become a part of you - familiar. It's a difficult problem with one solution — choose!

Study the word. Invest in it while it invests in you. Come to a wholeness with the word and it will become a part of you. Your very nature and you'll be able to use it (more effectively). More in the essence of love and creativity. More in line of doing what he asked you to do — be fruitful and multiply ... fill the earth (with his glory) and subdue it.

Commit your time and strength, amongst your means, to the truth of him. Good faith always comes in the pursuit. An interesting quote speaks, "Spend time gaining strength and you'll be strong enough to reach the summit (the victory). "

Things to know and do:

What has given you purpose?
Dedicate yourself to the cause.
Put action behind your words (works) faith.

Prayer:

Lord, Father reveal me to me. Then show through me the possibilities that I may see what to become. God I glorify you. I trust you and your word that my commitment is met with commitment for my good. On that I lean as I discover ways to serve and abide in you.

In Jesus name, I ask you to show me how to rely on you. Thanking you because I know it's done and
Amen.

More of Him

2nd Kings 19:31 | Psalm 37:5 | Psalm 105:8 | Proverbs 16:3 | Isaiah 56:4-8

Pray

Yet, Lord my God, give attention to your servant's prayer and his plea for mercy.
Hear the cry and the prayer that your servant is praying in your presence.
2nd Chronicles 6:19 (NIV)

✳ ✳ ✳

Have you had a conversation with God? A frank discussion about your circumstances and what can be done with them. You know he offers you peace and security throughout all your days. Is that what you have now? If you find that missing, then call on him at once.

Promises are no good if they aren't exercised and brought forward. Speak to God and more importantly speak with God and discover a true vision for your life. You might be missing out.

Without a doubt, you are, in fact (of some good things). But it's when troubles weigh on you that you notice (what you're missing). You really lean in for a conversation then. And that can be avoided or lessened — the trouble I mean; with a simple word from God. A word that can only come through (be received by) prayer.

Have an honest conversation with the Lord. (There's a song - Have a little Talk with Jesus, tell him all about our trouble)… He will hear — more importantly, He will answer.

Things to know and do:

Talk to God.

Listen to/ for God's reply.

Be real with yourself. (What is your truth?)

Prayer:

Lord, you are the reason I believe. Align me with your vision.
I am equipped with your strength and courage. I am full of the
knowledge of you. Direct me to where I may be of use that your
power may flow through me for your people.

In Jesus name,
Amen.

More of Him

1st Kings 9:3 | 2nd Chron. 6:19 | Job 33:26 | Luke 11:1 | Eph. 6:18 |
Philippians 4:6 | 1st Thess. 5:17

Persist

One day Jesus told his disciples a story to show that they should always pray and never give up. Luke 18:1 (NLT)

* * *

How much do you really want or need his promises? Are you willing to go all in and through to pursue them? Even if that means you have "no Life" beside your pursuit?

Sometimes that's what's required to see faith bear fruit in your life. Forsaking and surrendering all others to find a contentment in Him - in His word over your life. Do you have the faith to pursue (that) Him? I think you do because it was given to you. It was given to each person a measure of faith we simply have to use.

Dig in and go for it. Be dogged in your pursuit of all the things God has in store for you here. You may have much awaiting you in heaven but until the race finishes you have a course to run Here. And faith in an inexhaustive supply if you push for it. Pursue it with all abandon and you will find your supply line.

Remember if you're really after something, you have to dedicate (spend) resources to get it.

Things to know and do:

How bad do you want the gift?

What are you willing to do for the gift?

What do you want to gain and grow from this?

Prayer:

Heavenly Father, Great God of all things — heaven and earth belong to you as does all the health and wellness of the land. Give me strength, I pray, to pursue and meet your daily desires and goals as set for me. May I be empowered to handle all the darts that come my way with grace and poise as direct gifts from your hand.
I ask for this,
In Jesus Name in who I pray.
Amen.

More of Him

1st Samuel 1:7-11 | Job 7:11 | Psalm 40:1-3 | Psalm 102:4,42 | Romans 12:12 | Ephesians 6:18 | James 5:7-11

Devote

For we have become partners with Christ, if in fact we hold our initial confidence firm until the end. Hebrews 3:14 (NET)

* * *

How bad must you really want to change? Can you, do you, hold on to his word when things look a mess? When everything counterintuitively says give up; are you able to push through? I ask you to be dogged in your pursuit; but be just as dogged (hungry) in your faith — in your carrying the truth.

This is where your reminder, your daily push comes into play. When things look their bleakest "lo I am with you always." And as a boosting reminder, "even till the end of the world (the age)." Come what may, I have been through it and will walk you through it — just focus on me. That's what his abiding promise is about.

That's what he offers to us. Gifts, yes. Hope, yes! Someone who'll be there when you arrive or if you never arrive. He's right there with you.

If you're willing and able to see through this light momentary affliction.

Things to know and do:

Be confident in your decision.

Fix your faith (your vision) on what's good.

Pursue it with all diligence.

Prayer:

Great God, Our Father; thank you for all your provision in my life. Thank you for extending your hand of mercy and grace. For giving me your son for lending your son for the salvation of the world. I lean and rely on you for my comforts and my life. Lord bless me with more than intimate knowledge of you to share with others who seek to know your name and your face.
In Jesus name I Pray.
Amen.

More of Him

Genesis 5:24 | Psalm 27:13 | Psalm 86:13 | Daniel 1:8-17 | Hebrews 5:7 | Hebrews 11:1 | 2nd Corinthians 4:18

Assert Yourself

Do not fear them or their words, son of man. Though you will dwell among the thistles and briars of their hostility, though their reactions will make you think you're sitting on scorpions, do not be afraid. Pay no attention to their threats, and don't let their glaring faces intimidate you. Ezekiel 2:6 (VOICE)

＊ ＊ ＊

You are in charge. Metaphorically speaking, you have a say in what happens to you. Insist on getting the best. Don't get the idea wrong now — I don't mean the great delicacies and "beautiful" truths of the world. I mean the counter. Speak the actual written truth. Speak what God says about the situation. Find your word in Him.

He says there is no need to fear — there is no need to fear. He says subdue it. Subdue it! What God speaks is your authority to reach it; speak it — see it come to pass. You simply have to find agreement with Him — believe Him.

Take your place as owner — Take ownership of and do something about the problems and situations.

Things to know and do:

Exercise your God-given authority.

Make a decision and commit to it.

Be humble yet definitive.

Prayer:

Gracious Father, I pray that you would give me the wisdom to know what is mine and for me. To pursue it with all diligence and integrity. And to stand with the authority you have given me - to tread on serpents and scorpions and face down all the power of the enemy (my enemy) - the enemy of faith.

In Jesus Name I pray.
Amen.

More of Him

Psalm 91:13 | Psalm 110:1 | Luke 10:19 |Romans 1:16 | Galatians 4:1-7 |

Embolden Your Words

If I say, "my foot is slipping," your loyal love, O Lord, supports me. When worries
threaten to overwhelm me, your soothing touch makes me happy.
Psalm 49:18, 19 (NET)

* * *

It's impossible to know the real you without knowing the REAL
you. The hidden figure nobody knows except your maker - the
designer. Where there are weaknesses we often won't see unto
their revealed by choice or circumstance. God promises though to
uplift you. He promises to mold you into the person you should
be. He Promises to make you. And for that he uses his word. Using
specific verses, you too can find yourself in the text and let the
word empower you — embolden you to further exploits.

Speak it (the word) to yourself when you feel threatened,
weakened, or even at a loss.

Delight yourself (find the joy) in the law as you become
comfortable with the law and the prophets and promises of what
God offers — what the law says about you. Not the condemnation
but the helpful situations many others have been through and
came through — overcoming. "By the word of their testimony and
the blood of the Lamb."

Things to know and do:

Whose word do you believe?
Trust God – Trust His process.
Reach higher in order to go up further.

Prayer:

Heavenly Father, I look up to you because you are higher than every situation I face. When doubt and uncertainty come upon me, I reach for you. I call and more importantly I draw from the well of your word that you have never left me (never leave me) or forsaken me. That you will never leave me without hope or comfortless.

Bring me a spirit - your spirit of refreshing as only you can that I may be strengthened and encouraged to go/ pursue on.

In Jesus name I ask and I prayerfully receive.
Amen.

More of Him

Joshua 1:9 | Psalm 118:8 | Psalm 119: 92 | Pro. 3:26 | Pro. 12:25|
Romans 15:4 | Hebrews 6:18

Trust

... Think back and you will know without a doubt that not one single good thing that the Eternal One, your God, promised you has been left undone. Not a single one.
Joshua 23: 14 (Voice)
So trust in the Eternal One forever, for He is like a great Rock— strong, stable, trustworthy, and lasting. Isaiah 26:4 (VOICE)

* * *

Think about the person who shares your hopes and dreams. Most often we lean and rely on them especially when we encounter difficult circumstances. We call on them and for us they are the embodiment of fulfillment (the source). You could say they are where you place your hope and in whom you place your trust. They are the embodiment of God. He is ultimately the source of your strength, your anchor. God, by his spirit, is your wisdom and guidance. Your well-being is in His life. His that is to say Christ's life. Do you truly lean on him?

Do you believe he has faced what you're going to face? What you're presently facing and made it through to the other side. Let him then guide you there. Let his strength become your strength. His hope become your hope. Not meaning hope as in hope something happens and it's good fortune for me. Hope as in knowing what he says shall come to pass. In times prior you read that old saints knew and put forward the word, knowing with confidence in whom they were believing. The Lord is a rock (unshakeable — immoveable) use that as your foundation to pursue his promises. All them being yes and amen, take yes for an answer and go forward in the light of what he has called you.

Things to know and do:

Trust your decision.

Trust the vision.

Trust (him) on the outcome.

Prayer:

I believe! Help my unbelief.

More of Him

2nd Sam. 22:3 | 2nd Sam. 22:31 | Joshua 21:45 | Psalm 27:5 | Nahum 1:7 | Mark 9:24 | John 5:24

Live (In the Moment)

So then, do not worry about tomorrow, for tomorrow will worry about itself.
Today has enough trouble of its own.
Matthew 6:34 (NET)

* * *

This is the day the Lord has made. Let us rejoice and be full of glad tidings — and cheer. Forgetting the missteps of yesterday (Genesis 19:26), choosing instead to pursue (one faithful step at a time) the best decisions for today and tomorrow. Considering tomorrow but not letting it cloud your vision. Look at the good of the day there is to be done.

Look at the necessities of the moments around you. So many people have hurts. So many people have practical things of need. God has made you available to reach them on their level. And even your own receivership — awards being placed on a level you can see and appreciate. With the added bonus of gifts in heaven.

You receive from the word (Today). Give from the word (Today). Don't withhold your giving - don't worry about accumulation for tomorrows wealth is a promise that can only be experienced when it is reached.

Things to know and do:

Forget the past!
Weigh the future.
Choose to do good today.

Prayer:

Lord and Jesus,
I pray for only what I can hold. I know you promise never to put more on me than I can bear. Let me take in today's portion and only the days as I have my fill and you provide me with strength. Let me see what is good and necessary and teach me to provide it willingly and obediently as unto you in my brethren.

May I be of good use and firm commitment in the light and love this life provides me in faith through Christ Jesus,

In whose name and spirit I pray.
Amen.

More of Him

Psalm 118:17 | Psalm 118:24 | Luke 8:14 | Luke 10:30-36 | Luke 10:41, 42 | Phil. 4:6 | 1st Peter 5:7

Remember/ Remind /
Be Reminded

Remind me of what happened! Let's debate! You, prove to me that you are right!
Isaiah 43:26 (NET)

* * *

We look to the past for courage when facing a pressing situation. Visualizing the best of the memory for strength. Forgetting the difficulty or circumstances we've actually overcome — the triumphs. You would think if any experience could teach us to rely more on God, through faith, it would be found in the former. Yet God is doing a new thing.

In the history of it, let us draw forth a river of life. God has delivered us. God has brought us this far. Through God, all the best that has happened (even if it didn't appear so at the time) has happened in our life. It's important though to remember the process.

Recount the deeds of the past, especially of faith, they set a stage for today and tomorrow's hope. Look for great and minor victories and speak what God has promised and brought about. It is crucial to know and be comforted in the wait and sharing the building of faith with others. Remember God always delivers.

You may not be the one to see it. But your faith sees it and you must speak it as done.

Things to know and do:

Write the vision.
Preserve what God has spoken to you.
Speak it (what God has spoken to you).

Prayer:

Honor to you God Most High,
Hear my calls, my cries; my groans. Hear from heaven and answer me speedily. What I write, type, draw; be it print or spoken word — you promised to be with me. Lo, I am with you always. You promised to supply my need. According to your riches in glory in Christ Jesus. Make your promises to be revealed in me. Make your promise a vision for all to behold your glory in my life. In the life of all those who are truly your servants. Send your angel with their answer speedily. Make them to know from your spirit in this moment.

In Jesus name, I ask this prayer.
Amen.

More of Him

Genesis 9:16 | Deuteronomy 8:18 | Deuteronomy 32:4 | Psalm 119:49 | Micah 7:18, 19 | John 14:26

Be Humble/
Esteem Others

Don't let selfishness and prideful agendas take over. Embrace true humility, and lift your heads to extend love to others. Philippians 2:3 (VOICE)

* * *

Is your current view of you accurate? Is it real or you as you imagine yourself to be? How you answer, see yourself especially in the light of others and others view of you, is an important test to take. There are nerves exposed that prove quite sensitive to the touch. Yet they need to be to accurately see whether or not it is of true faith.

Ask yourself, do you seek answers for others or from them — on your behalf? Your needs are a priority, yes. But with God so is / are his other children. And your view of them reveals as much about you as it does them. Humility embodies putting others first.

To be clear, putting others first doesn't mean your needs aren't weighed. You can make them known but while you wait; find ways to meet the needs of those less fortunate.

God has promised you both a lifting up. God has promised to provide you both with a change. Be the change others need that God/ and God - will supply the change you need.

Things to know and do:

Consider the needs of others.

Identify what moves you.

Humility is a service not servitude.

Prayer:

Heavenly Father, Holy and Reverent is your name above names, Lord Jehovah. Help me forgo my pride and envy, greed and self-conceit as you build a faithful character in me. Show me the ways I grieve your spirit and his work. And heal me! Heal me that I may see others as you see them, in their need and where I can assist them through you. Give me your servant's heart with a master's wisdom

In Jesus Name I pray,
Lord, Amen!

More of Him

Genesis 41:16 | 1st Samuel 2:7 | Proverbs 15:33 | Romans 12:3 | Philippians 2:6-9 |Ephesians 5:21

Give Beyond

It is possible to give away and become richer! It is also possible to hold on too tightly and lose everything. Yes, the liberal man shall be rich! By watering others, he waters himself. Proverbs 11:25 (TLB)

* * *

Giving is a rich opportunity to share faith. Rich because it increases the wealth of the giver more than all the gifts that are received. Some see it as an act of worship and it is. It's an act of adoration an expression of a higher state of being. The humility of putting something (someone) other, first.

The other in question is God. Even as you share with your fellow man. Spiritually you're giving to God or gods. Depending on where your dollar goes. Please forgive the anecdote because the gift is so much more than money.

Suffice it to say, giving God or even to God is your first priority in giving. God through his man (men). God through his causes and circumstances. God in the sharing of his word with those who lack — who need. Giving is the promise that gives to you. A godly decision with repercussions that are always for the giver's good. Giving and sacrificing at the altar of redemption, offering, growth, resurrection. These things are possible because of a gift. God gave his (only begotten) son. And coming from a gracious heart the gift and the giving are united. Give from the word as you receive from the word and you maintain the flow of the word — from God to the people. A popular saying goes, "Withhold not your giving awaiting accumulation — if it's going to happen it will happen after you empty yourself to create space". This applies both to friends and enemies.

Things to know and do:

Giving is a decision.

The gift is as important as the giver.

Give God (Put God) first.

Prayer:

Gracious Lord, you provide everything our hands are stretched to profit and gain, everything we need; everything we ask for in your son name. We thank you for your pouring out and pouring in your people — those who richly deserve it or need a helping hand. Lord it is for your glory that we benefit and remain beneficial to the preservation of this earth for this time until your time is come. Keep us, keep me, in your cupboard to be poured out as you see fit — when you see fit; till the kingdom comes.

In Jesus name I pray,
Amen.

More of Him

Proverbs 28:27 | Matthew 5:40-44 | Mark 10:44 | Luke 6:38 |
Luke 10:30-35 | Hebrews 13:16 |

See the Author

I will lift up my eyes to the hills, from where does my help come? My help comes from the Lord, who made heaven and earth. Psalm 121:1, 2 (MEV)

* * *

Recognition means reaching.

Reaching a level of comfortability or familiarity with something or someone. It takes some doing to get to that point but it's worth it. Especially of faith, because it establishes history — a working relationship. David knew God; saw God as higher. Therefore he looked up (and to God) when he needed help.

Even when falling on our face to pray, we're looking to someone, for someone higher than ourselves. What we lack in sufficiency to handle the problem - God promises to supply all of our NEED. Everything! Simply focus on him. Turn to (rely on) him because he is reliable. He is the source — of all comfort; all rest. The answer to the pending situation is — what does God have to say about it. Put your faith in a seed of what he's already done. That's what he'll continue to do and more. Growing to strengthen and encourage you.

Things to know and do:

Fix your gaze.
Focus your strength.
Envision your future.

Prayer:

Heavenly Father, Most High God
Reveal to me my innermost character being. My hidden spiritual
truth, if it's unlike you or not in your image, correct me so that I
may be on the journey you would have me on. Teach me to trust
and rely on you as my source and guide for all things pertaining
to godliness, holiness and wholeness in thy being Christ Jesus.
Teach me to see as you see — this world, by faith and with faith;
trusting in you and your decisions about what's best. Allow
me to develop the love and caring you share with the world —
shared with the world in Jesus Christ.

In whose name I pray.
Amen.

More of Him

1st Samuel 24:18, 19 | Isaiah 40: 28, 29 | Isaiah 41:13 | Psalm 36:7 |
Psalm 130:5 | Micah 7:7 |

With Thanks

* * *

The author and publisher would like to thank you for your interest in this publication. May the faith-filled words aid you in your Journey, bless and keep you in God's peace and under his glory. In addition to the 14 inspirational thoughts we've included an additional devotion as well a preview of new and other releases available from the Life in Print Media Group.

Bible Copyright(s)

Certain materials were essential in developing this publication.

Draw Closer

It is good for me to be near you. I choose you as my protector, and I will tell about your wonderful deeds. Psalm 73:28 (CEV)

* * *

Relationships. The key to faith and trusting God.

Everything is relative but you are, (what's) the more important, because he created you. He designed you. He breathed in you his breath. And furthermore wants to connect with you. Are you ready to reach out (to him)?

Drawing closer to the promise and the promiser means finding togetherness. And that is the idea faith is after. Bringing God and you to one accord. The agreement — the partnership… Wisdom and faith — trusting in the knowledge of him and believing he cares for you.

We being interconnected. All life comes from him and returns to him. Drawing near; nearness means empowerment; empowering you to go further; push harder for growth in him (in the word). The more you discover about the word - the more you discover about him. The more you discover about him the more you'll discover about your true nature and selves. Those that draw nigh

45

to God in a way of duty shall find God pulling them close in a way of mercy. Draw nigh to him in faith, and trust, and obedience, and he will draw nigh to you for your deliverance. If there be not a close communion between God and us, it is our flaw, and not his because his hand remains outstretched.

Let today be a reminder. There are friends who are friends, and there is a friend that wants to be and is closer than a brother.

Things to know and do:

Partner with the invisible to see the impossible.
Commit to building and maintaining healthy relationships.
Follow up and follow through.

Prayer:

God in whose holiness is perfect, God in whom heaven fears and worships, God who is whole and complete, draw me in that I may be complete with you. That I may find rest and comfort in your arms through your son and eternal spirit. You call me and teach me to answer that I may give me (myself) and receive you. Your blessing. Your gift. The eternal life in Christ Jesus.

In whose name I pray this prayer,
Thank you God - Amen!

More of Him

2nd Chron. 15:2 | Proverbs 18:24 | Isaiah 58:2 | Luke 21:28 | Romans 13:11 | Hebrews 10:22 | James 4:8

Before you go
Don't forget to check out our other release(s):

Exploring the Five Senses
A World of Faith in Focus

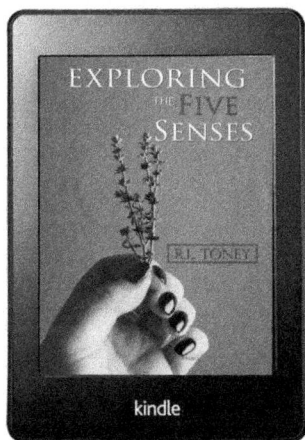

Available in Print and Electronic Media

Faith is a much discussed topic. Many guides seek to unveil the mystery of its workings. This is your practical guide to seeing, experiencing, the power of faith at work for you.

Exploring the Five Senses is a new journey in the tangible workings of believing and growing - developing the spiritual strength; to change your life forever.

Wake Your Faith Up
14 Days Praying the Promises of God

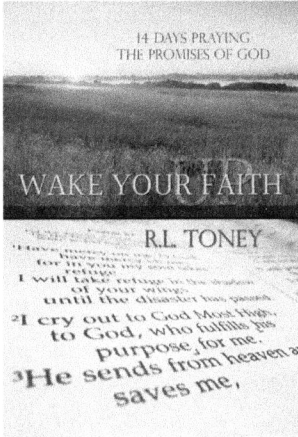

Available in Print and Electronic Media

This quick reader is your personal 14 day plan to transform your today into the tomorrow you know it can be. Using the authority of the Word and the power of believing, learn to express your faith daily over any situation and witness the change — see life bear the fruit He promised you from the beginning.

Wake your faith up!

Shake up the complacency of wanting to and be what he called you to. Less than a moment a day for the next 14 days, feed the desire and sow a bountiful harvest toward your faith. Record your journey each day and find yourself empowered to do all He said you can do.

Get Your Copy Today

Read more and see other releases at Life in Print Media
www.lifeinprint.org

Author Profile

Richard R.L. Toney is the "voice behind the pen" publishing (The Lion's Well - Inspirational Journal) as well as other print and online offerings. At the center of his writings is a simple yet powerful statement of faith.

> "Everybody has faith but it's not always dependable where you place it"

Founder of the Life in Print Media Group, R.L. is a shepherd of the CN Life Foundation - a local empowerment initiative in the southern United States.

He is a young voice with a lengthy passion for the power of the word. Prior to the ministry, his studies in the arts laid a foundation of how the word connects the world. In language and text, he often quotes "A word is the source of every deed, a thought every action." Of faith he writes, "If you can't trust the word - it can never empower you to act."

It is this message as speaker and publisher he shares in his works.

Available online at your favorite retailer as well as
www.rltoney.com

You are urged, if you found this publication enlightening or helpful, to see what more is available from this and other authors being published at www.lifeinprint.org

Come by today and see where this growing life connection can take you!

www.ingramcontent.com/pod-product-compliance
Lightning Source LLC
Chambersburg PA
CBHW060055050426
42448CB00011B/2478